G000136157

Ramadan Guide

Book 2024

A Comprehensive Guide to Fasting, Praying, and Enjoying the Holy Month of Ramadan

Habiba Abdul-Rahman

Table of Contents

INTRODUCTION

Ramadan is the ninth month of the Islamic lunar calendar and the holiest month for Muslims. It is the month when Muslims believe Allah gave the Quran, the sacred book of Islam, to Prophet Muhammad via the angel Gabriel. This event is called the **Night of the Power or Laylat al-Qadr**.

During Ramadan, Muslims fast from sunrise until sunset, foregoing food, drink, and other pleasures. Fasting is one of Islam's five pillars, or fundamental acts of devotion that all Muslims should do. Fasting benefits Muslims by purifying their spirits, increasing thankfulness, and strengthening their **faith.**

Ramadan is a time for spiritual meditation, prayer, charity, and fellowship. Muslims read and recite the Quran, offer additional prayers at night, donate liberally to the destitute, and enjoy meals with their loved ones. Ramadan celebrates Allah's guidance, benevolence, and **forgiveness**.

Ramadan concludes with the Eid al-Fitr holiday, which translates as "the feast of breaking the fast". On this day, Muslims praise Allah for

Ramadan's bounties, exchange presents, and enjoy celebratory food and activities.

PREPARING FOR RAMADAN

Making the most of this fortunate month of fasting, prayer, and almsgiving may be achieved by being ready for Ramadan. Here are some pointers on how to be ready for Ramadan in many ways:

Goal-Setting and Intention-Setting

Before the start of Ramadan, it's important to establish specific, attainable objectives and aspirations for the month. For example, you could want to study the complete Quran, provide more charity, recite the Taraweeh prayers, or work on your character. Make sure your objectives are clear, quantifiable, doable, relevant, and time-bound, regardless of what they are. Additionally, ensure that your motives are pure and only for Allah's benefit—not for attention or approval from others.

Scheduling your Time and Activities

To reach your objectives, you must arrange your daily schedule and activities. This is the first step in setting goals and intentions. To fit your fasting and worship schedule, you may need to make adjustments to your job, study, family, and social obligations. It can also be necessary for you to assign or put off the less urgent chores and give priority to the more crucial ones. For task and time management, you may use an app, a calendar, or a planner. To keep track of your development and celebrate your successes, you may also keep a Ramadan notebook.

Creating a Ramadan Checklist

This is a useful tool that will assist you in practically preparing for Ramadan. It may include things like:

- Buying plenty of wholesome, easily prepared food and beverages for suhoor and iftar.
- Decluttering and embellishing your house to foster a joyous and spiritual ambiance.
- Trying to pay your bills and zakat before the beginning of Ramadan.
- Completing, if appropriate, any Ramadan fasts neglected.
- Asking Allah's forgiveness as well as the forgiveness of anybody you may have harmed or insulted.
- Compiling a list of those you want to see or invite to Iftar or Eid.
- Compiling a list of organizations or causes you want to assist or give to during Ramadan.

- Make a list of the books, films, podcasts, talks, and novels you want to watch or listen to throughout Ramadan.

Looking for wisdom and motivation

You have a wonderful chance to learn more about Islam and its teachings throughout Ramadan. To do this, consider reading and reciting the Quran aloud, either with or without translation and commentary, and making an effort to comprehend and implement its teachings into your daily life.

- One way to learn about numerous issues linked to Ramadan and Islam is to watch or attend lectures, seminars, or webinars given by credible experts and speakers.
- Starting or joining a book club or study group with your family or friends to talk about and share the lessons you've learned.
- Maintaining a social media presence or subscribing to blogs, newsletters, or other accounts that provide reliable and practical resources, advice, and information about Islam during Ramadan.

FASTING IN RAMADAN

As one of the five pillars of Islam, fasting throughout the month of Ramadan is a religious obligation for Muslims. It's a month dedicated to introspection, prayer, almsgiving, and fellowship. During a fast, one must refrain from eating, drinking, and enjoying other pleasures from sunrise until sunset. For those unable to fast for medical or other reasons, there are a few allowances and exemptions. In this life as well as the next, fasting offers a lot of advantages and rewards; yet, there are drawbacks as well as remedies. Some spiritual and physical practices, such as reading the Quran, praying more, giving alms, asking for pardon, and making supplications, might improve fasting.

Fasting Rules and Etiquette

The requirements that Muslims adhere to fast decently and courteously are known as the fasting rules and etiquette. A few guidelines and customs around fasting include:

- **Intentionally Fasting:** During the month of Ramadan, Muslims are required to intend to fast each night before the morning prayer. To fast for Allah's sake and to seek His reward, one must abstain from acts that invalidate the fast. Muslims are prohibited from eating, drinking, smoking, having sex, purposely vomiting, menstruating, or bleeding while giving birth. This declaration comes from the heart, not the tongue.

- **Avoiding sins with the tongue**: Muslims must also abstain from saying or acting in a way that angers Allah, such as lying, backbiting, cursing, arguing, or gossiping. These behaviors render the fast void and necessitate making up the lost day or paying a fine. These behaviors lessen or sometimes completely negate the benefits of the fast. According to the Prophet Muhammad (peace be upon him), "Allah does not require that anyone give up food or drink if they do not give up false speech, acting upon it, and ignorance.

- **Breaking the Fast at the Appropriate Time**: To emulate the Prophet Muhammad (peace be upon him), Muslims need to break their fast as soon as the sun sets. The Prophet said: The people will remain on the right path as long as they hasten the breaking of the fast.

- **Avoiding Overeating or Indulging in Unhealthy Foods:** Muslims should break the fast moderately and healthily, and refrain from filling their stomachs with food or drink. - Breaking the fast is recommended to be done by drinking water or eating an odd number of dates, followed by the sunset prayer. **"The son of Adam does not fill any vessel worse than his stomach,"** said the Prophet Muhammad (peace be upon him). To sustain himself, the son of Adam just has to consume a few mouthfuls. If he is forced to do so, allow him to fill three-quarters of his stomach with air, water, and food." Foods that are very hot, salty, or fried should also be avoided by Muslims since they might make them more thirsty or induce indigestion.

- **Sincere fasting for Allah's Benefit**: Fasting should be done by Muslims out of devotion and sincerity, not to impress or appease others. All acts of the son of Adam are for Allah, the Exalted and Majestic, except fasting, according to the Prophet Muhammad (peace be upon him). It is intended (just) for Me, and I (alone) will give it recompense. A barrier is fast. When one of you observes a fast day, he should not use profanity or get angry; instead, he should respond, "I am a person fasting," to anybody who mocks him or attempts to argue with him."

These are some guidelines and customs related to fasting that Muslims need to be aware of and respect. Muslims who adhere to them will reap the blessings of fasting in this life as well as the next.

The Advantages and Benefits of Fasting

Muslims who fast experience a strengthening of their faith, an increase in thankfulness, and a purification of their souls1. Muslims who fast also learn self-control, discipline, charity, and patience. Additionally, fasting improves blood pressure, cholesterol, blood sugar, and weight control, among other health benefits. According to the Prophet Muhammad (peace be upon him), Muslims who fast also get large rewards from Allah: "Every deed of the son of Adam will be multiplied, with a good deed receiving a tenfold to seven hundredfold reward." "Except fasting, which is done for Me and for which I will reward you because you give up your passion and food for Me," said Allah, the Almighty and Majestic.

Common Problems with Fasting and how to solve them

Ramadan may be difficult, particularly if it comes in the summer or an area with extended daylight hours. The following are some typical issues with fasting and their fixes:

- **Hunger and Thirst**: These are physiological sensations that put a fasting person's resolve to the test. Eating a healthy, well-balanced pre-dawn meal (suhur), drinking plenty of water both before and after fasting, and avoiding salty, spicy, or fried meals that might make you thirstier are some ways to deal with them. Together with seeking Allah's assistance and mercy, one should keep in mind the benefits and purposes of fasting.

- **Weakness and Fatigue**: These are typical outcomes of fasting, particularly during the first days of Ramadan. Getting enough sleep, napping throughout the day, and avoiding physically demanding activities are the best ways to combat them. When breaking the fast (iftar), one should also consume nutritious and invigorating items such as fruits, vegetables, grains, and proteins. To increase spiritual vigor and drive, one should also recite the Quran, offer up prayers, and make requests.

- **Dehydration and Headache**: These are potential side effects of fasting, particularly if the person is dehydrated or has not had enough caffeine before the fast. They may be avoided by drinking enough water and other liquids both before and after fasting, as well as by cutting down on or progressively stopping caffeine before Ramadan.

In addition, one should keep their nose moistened with a humidifier or nasal spray and stay out of the heat, bright sunshine, and loud noises. After breaking the fast, one might take medicine or see a doctor if the headache is severe or prolonged.

Spiritual and Physical Benefits of Fasting

Fasting is a spiritual as well as a physical practice. As a result, the following advice should be followed to maximize the advantages of fasting for both the soul and the body:

- **Reading and Reciting the Quran**: Ramadan is the month of the Quran, which is the message of Allah. As a result, during Ramadan, one should endeavor to read and recite the whole Quran as often as feasible. In addition, one should make an effort to comprehend the meaning and lessons found in the Quran and apply them to their own lives.

- **Offering Additional Prayers**: During Ramadan, in addition to the five required prayers, one should offer additional prayers such as the duha (forenoon prayers), taraweeh (night prayers), and anqiyasam (late night prayers).

- **Charitable Giving**: Among Islam's finest actions, charitable giving is particularly recommended during Ramadan. It also increases one's reward and sense of closeness to Allah. Charity should be given to the underprivileged, the destitute, orphans, refugees, and other worthy individuals. In addition, if one fulfills the requirements, one should provide the required charity (zakat) and the charity of breaking the fast (fitrana) after Ramadan. Giving shields from the hellfire and cleanses the heart and money.

- **Seeking Forgiveness**: If someone fasts and repents genuinely, Allah will pardon their misdeeds; so, Ramadan is a month of forgiveness. As a result, one should constantly ask Allah for forgiveness as well as the forgiveness of everyone they may have hurt or offended. In addition, they need to make amends and provide forgiveness to those who have hurt or offended them.

- **Making Supplications**: Supplications are the expression of one's needs, wants, and ambitions to Allah. Forgiveness purifies the soul and offers serenity and happiness. Allah hears from His slaves with great pleasure and grants their requests. As a result, it is recommended that prayers be said to Allah often, particularly before the morning prayer, throughout the last ten nights of Ramadan, and at the times of breaking the fast.

Additionally, one needs to offer prayers for oneself, one's friends, family, neighborhood, and the whole Muslim ummah. In addition to providing consolation and solace, prayers deepen our relationship and faith with Allah.

PRAYING DURING RAMADAN

Praying during Ramadan is an essential act of devotion for Muslims since it is one of the five pillars of Islam. It is a means of speaking with Allah, asking for forgiveness, guidance, and mercy, as well as expressing thanks, adoration, and love for Him. Here are some suggestions to assist you in comprehendingperformingerform your Ramadan prayers:

The Necessity and Qualities of Prayer

Prayer is the most significant and beneficial action for a Musli since it will be the first question answered on the Day of Judgment. The Prophet Muhammad (peace be upon him) stated, "The first item to be assessed among a person's acts on the Day of Resurrection is prayer. If something is in excellent condition, he will thrive and flourish; if it is faulty, he will fail and lose." Prayer also shields a Muslim against sin and evil, as Allah states in the Quran: "Indeed, prayer prohibits immorality and wrongdoing." (29:45) Prayer also offers serenity and calm to the heart and spirit, as Allah states: "Those who have believed and whose hearts are secured by the remembrance of Allah. Without a doubt, the remembrance of Allah assures hearts." (13:28)

The Mandatory and Optional Prayers

Muslims are obligated to do five mandatory prayers every day, at certain times and in a specific way. These include the morning prayer (fajr), midday prayer (zuhr), afternoon prayer (asr), sunset prayer (maghrib), and night prayer (isha). These prayers form the foundation of the day and night, as well as the minimal need for a Muslim. Muslims are also urged to do voluntary prayers, which are additional prayers that may be performed at any time except for periods when prayer is prohibited, such as dawn, sunset, and midday. These prayers are intended to increase the reward and closeness to Allah while also compensating for any faults in the required ones. Voluntary prayers include the two units before fajr, the four units before zuhr and the two units after it, the two units after maghrib, and the two units after isha.

The Special Prayers of Ramadan: Taraweeh and Qiyam

The Taraweeh is a night prayer performed in the congregation after the isha prayer, and it may be eight or twenty units long, according to the imam's preference. Taraweeh is a manner of reciting and listening to the Quran, and it is customary to read the whole Quran during Ramadan prayers. The Taraweeh also has a significant reward and virtue, as the Prophet Muhammad (peace be upon him) stated: "Whoever prays during the night in Ramadan with faith and seeking reward from Allah will have his past sins forgiven." The qiyam is a late-night prayer performed in the last part of the night before the morning prayer. It may have any number of units depending on the individual's ability and time restrictions. The qiyam is a technique of begging Allah's forgiveness and guidance, especially during the last ten nights of Ramadan, when the Night of Power (Laylat al-Qadr) occurs. The qiyam is also rich in reward and virtue, as the Prophet Muhammad (peace be upon him) declared: "Whoever stands (in prayer) in Laylat al-Qadr out of faith and in the hope of reward, his previous sins will be forgiven.

The Etiquettes and Tips for Prayer

Muslims follow prayer etiquettes and recommendations for proper and polite performance. Some of them are:

- **Self-purification and Prayer Location**: Muslims should do ablution (wudu) before each prayer, which consists of washing their hands, mouth, nose, face, arms, head, ears, and feet with water. Muslims should also dress modestly and pray in a clean and peaceful setting, facing the Kaaba in Mecca (qiblah).

- **Intention and Concentration**: Muslims should pray for Allah's sake alone, not to impress or satisfy others. Muslims should also focus on the content and words of the prayer, avoiding any distractions or notions that may divert their attention away from Allah.

- **Adhering to the Sunnah and Etiquette of the Prophet Muhammad (peace be upon him):** Muslims should follow the Prophet Muhammad's (peace be upon him) example and direction in prayer, including time, gestures, recitations, and supplications. Muslims should also follow the Prophet Muhammad's (peace be upon him) etiquette before, during, and after prayer, including humility, respect, kindness, and thankfulness.

READING THE QURAN IN RAMADAN

The History and Revelation of the Quran

The Quran is Allah's last and complete revelation to humanity, and it serves as Muslims' principal source of guidance and regulation. It is divided into 114 chapters (surahs) and 6,236 verses (ayahs) that address a wide range of issues including religion, worship, morality, history, law, and science. The Quran was progressively revealed over 23 years, beginning in 610 CE, when Prophet Muhammad (peace be upon him) was 40 years old, and ending in 632 CE. The first revelation happened during Ramadan when he was meditating in the Cave of Hira near Mecca. The angel Gabriel appeared to him and said, "Read in the name of your Lord, Who created man from a clot of blood. Read, and your Lord is the most generous, who taught man what he did not know via the writing." (96:1-5) This signaled the start of his prophethood and the rise of Islam. The Night of Power (Laylat al-Qadr) is considered one of the most important and fortunate evenings for Muslims. Allah states in the Quran, "We sent it down on a blessed night: We have always sent warnings." (44:3) as well. "The Night of Decree is better than a thousand months." (97:3)

The Quran was revealed in Arabic, the language of the Prophet (peace be upon him) and his followers, and it has survived in its original form and language to this day. The Prophet (peace be upon him) and his companions learned the Quran, which was also inscribed on parchment, bones, and leaves. The Quran was assembled into a single book under the caliphate of Abu Bakr, the Prophet's first successor (peace be upon him), and it was standardized and disseminated during the caliphate of Uthman, the Prophet's third successor. The Topkapi Manuscript in Turkey, the Sana'a Manuscript in Yemen, and the Birmingham Manuscript in theUK[3] are among the earliest manuscripts of the Quran held in museums and libraries worldwide.

Reading the Quran during Ramadan is a highly recommended and fulfilling form of devotion for Muslims since it is the month when the Quran is revealed. Muslims seek to recite and listen to the Quran as often as possible, to complete it at least once throughout Ramadan. They also attempt to comprehend and apply the lesson to their life. Reading the Quran throughout Ramadan provides several advantages and blessings, including gaining Allah's pleasure and forgiveness, improving one's knowledge and intelligence, and mending one's spirit and body.

Benefits and Advantages of Reading the Quran

Some of the benefits and advantages of reading the Quran include:

- It is a way of gaining Allah's love and forgiveness, as Allah states, "And when you recite the Quran, We establish a secret barrier between you and those who do not believe in the Hereafter. And We have put covers over their hearts so that they do not comprehend, as well as deafness in the ears. And when you mention your Lord alone in the Quran, people recoil in horror." (17:45-46)

- According to Allah, "This is the Book (the Quran), whereof there is no doubt, guidance to those who are Al-Muttaqoon [the pious]" (2:2) along with "And We have certainly given you, [O Muhammad], seven of the often repeated [verses] and the great Quran." (15:87)

- It is healing and kindness, as Allah says, "And We send down the Quran that is healing and mercy for the believers, but it does not increase the wrongdoers except in loss." (17:82) and mercy: "O mankind, there has to come to you instruction from your Lord and healing for what is in the breasts and guidance and mercy for the believers." (10:57)

- It is a criterion and a light, as Allah says, "The month of Ramadan [is that] in which was revealed the Quran, a guidance for the people, and clear proofs of guidance and criterion." (2:185) It says "O mankind, there has come to you a conclusive proof from your Lord, and We have sent down to you a clear light." According to the Prophet (peace be upon him), the Quran serves as both a witness and an intercessor on the Day of Resurrection. Recite the two luminous ones, al-Baqarah and Al 'Imran, since on the Day of Resurrection, they will appear as two clouds, two shadows, or two flocks of birds in rows, begging for those who recite them. Recite Surah al-Baqarah, because using it is a blessing, and giving it up is a source of anguish, and magicians cannot deal with it."

The Techniques and Tools for Comprehending the Quran

The techniques and tools for comprehending the QuraMany approaches may utilized to interpret the Quran, including:

Tafsir is the science of explaining and understanding the Quran using its context, language, history, and sources. Tafsir clarifies the meanings, ramifications, and applications of the Quranic texts. Tafsir of the Quran is available in several books and websites, including [Tafsir Ibn Kathir], [Tafsir al-Jalalayn], and [Quran.com].

- **Translation**: The process of translating the Quran from Arabic to another language, such as English, Urdu, French, etc. Translation helps non-Arabic speakers understand the Quran's overall meaning and essential principles. However, translation cannot convey the entire beauty, eloquence, and clarity of the Quranic language, and it may have restrictions and faults. As a result, the translation should be utilized in conjunction with, rather than in instead of, the original Quran. Several versions of the Quran are accessible online and in print, including [The Clear Quran], [The Noble Quran], and [The Quran: A New Translation].

Tajweed is the technique of reciting the Quran with proper pronunciation, intonation, and Arabic language standards. Tajweed helps to maintain the precision, clarity, and melody of Quranic recitation. Tajweed also improves comprehension and appreciation for Quranic language and tones. There are several resources and courses available for learning Quranic tajweed, including [Tajweed Rules], [Learn Quran Tajweed], and [Quranic].

Tips and Techniques for Memorizing the Quran

- **Aim**: The first and most crucial suggestion is to memorize the Quran with the true aim of seeking Allah's favor and pleasure. Having a genuine aim will encourage and inspire one to memorize the Quran, making the process simpler and more beneficial.

- **Consistency**: The second advice is to memorize the Quran regularly One should create a daily or weekly timetable and adhere to it without missing or postponing. One should also choose a good time and location for remembering, ideally in the morning or after the dawn prayer, when the mind is fresh and alert, and in a calm and clean environment, such as a mosque or library.

- **Repetition**: The third suggestion is to read and study the Quran on a regular and systematic basis. Repeat the verses you're remembering multiple times until they're firmly engraved in your mind. One should also go over the previous passages that one has remembered and repeat them in prayers or to a teacher or companion. Use spaced repetition strategies, such as flashcards or apps, to strengthen learning and minimize forgetting.

- **Understanding**: The fourth guideline is to grasp and comprehend the Quran that you are memorizing. One should read the translation and tafsir of the verses they are memorizing to their meaning, message, and context. One should also contemplate and analyze the verses, attempting to apply them to one's life. Understanding the Quran will make memorizing more meaningful and pleasurable, as well as help you recall the verses more effectively.

- **Dua**: The piece of advice is to perform a dua and beg Allah for guidance and success in memorizing the Quran. One should own one's weakness and reliance on Allah, and seek His direction and support in studying and memorizing the Quran. One should also pray to Allah to make the Quran a source of illumination, guidance, and kindness for them in this world and the next.

GIVING DURING RAMADAN

The Obligation and Excellence of Zakat

One of the five pillars of Islam is zakat, which is the religious obligation of all Muslims who meet the qualifying requirements to donate a certain portion of their annual income to charitable causes. An excess of yearly profits for individuals and families is purified via zakat.

There are many benefits and rewards associated with zakat in this life as well as the next. Zakat offers many advantages and benefits, including:

- It is a means of gaining Allah's approval and pardon, as He states: "And establish prayer and give zakat; and whatever good you offer to Allah, He will find." Yes, Allah observes everything that you do. 2:110

- In the words of the Prophet Muhammad (peace be upon him), "Charity does not decrease wealth." It is a way to increase and purify one's possessions. [Muslim] stated "W, however, pays the zakat on his wealth will have its evil removed from him." The Ibn Majah. In the process of eradicating injustice, inequality, and poverty, it upholds the well-being and dignity of the underprivileged.

- It is an expression of gratitude and faith since it shows one's commitment to Allah and one's thankfulness for His blessings.

The Types and Recipients of Zakat

According to the Quran, there are eight categories in which respectable individuals or organizations fall under which they might get zakat. These are listed in the following order:

- The poor (al-fuqara), which translates to "low-income" or "destitute."
- The needy, also known as alal-maskinis a person in need.
- Zakat administrators (al-mailing alayha), distributors, and collectors of zakat.
- New Muslims and members of the Muslim community who need reconciliation of their hearts (al-muallafatu qulubuhum).
- Individuals in bondage (al-riqab), denoting enslaved people and captives who need release.
- The term "the debt-ridden" (al-gharimin) describes those who are unable to make their debt repayments.

- For the sake of Allah" (fi sabilillah) refers to those who, like mujahideen, scholars, and da'wah workers, strive and battle for Allah's sake.
- The wayfarer (ibn al-sabil), is a term used to describe a person who is lost or has little resources.

The following zakat categories and recipients should be observed and respected by Muslims. By giving zakat, Muslims may benefit from it both in this life and the next.

The Calculation and Distribution of Zakat

You must ascertain your nisab and your zakatable assets to compute zakat. The niqab is the minimal net worth that serves as a cutoff point to ascertain whether you are required to pay zakat. The market price determines the value of gold or silver, which is the basis for the niqab. You may determine the current nisab value using internet resources like [Zakat Calculator]. The wealth that is subject to zakat includes cash, gold, silver, stocks, business items, cattle, crops, and rental income. These are known as your zakatable assets. All of your zakatable assets must be valued, and any outstanding obligations or liabilities must be deducted. You must pay zakat on it if the net amount is more than or equal to the nisab. 2.5% is the zakat rate, which implies that you must pay 2.5% of your net zakatable worth in zakat.

To give zakat, you must first determine who qualifies for it. Allah lists these people in the Quran. The following eight groups of persons are eligible to receive zakat:

- The impoverished, or "Al-fuqara," who are unable to satisfy their fundamental demands due to their lack of resources.
- The needy, or "Al-maskin," which refers to those who are struggling and in need of help.
- The zakat collectors (Al-amilina alayha), who are designated to gather and distribute zakat on behalf of the government or the community.
- The "new converts" (Al-muallafatu qulubuhum), or those who are leaning toward Islam and in need of assistance or defense.
- The term "slaves," or "Al-niqab," refers to those who are held as slaves or captives and who need ransom payments or release.
- The debtors (Al-gharimin), or those in need of assistance or forgiveness because they are saddled with obligations they are unable to pay back.
- The wayfarers (Ibn Al-Al-Nabil who are migrants or travelers who are lost and in need of assistance.

- The cause of Allah (Fi sabadilla), refers to those who battle, study, or labor in the Islamic way to strive and struggle for Allah's cause.

You have two options for distributing your zakat: either directly to the qualified beneficiaries or via a reputable company like [Islamic Relief] or [Muslim Aid] that collects and distributes zakat on your behalf. Make sure your zakat is delivered to the rightful recipients in a timely and respectful way and that you get a receipt or proof of your donation.

The Recommended and Optional Charity

In addition to zakat, Muslims are also encouraged to give to other charitable causes, such as:

- **Sadaqah**: Any voluntary, all-encompassing good act performed for Allah's sake is referred to by this phrase. Sadaqah may be donated to anybody for any purpose, at any time, and in any quantity. Sadaqah may take many forms, such as cash, products, services, or even just a kind word or a smile. Sadaqah provides several advantages and rewards, including boosting one's income, atoning for transgressions, and shielding one from disasters.

- **Zakat Al-Fitr:** Every Muslim who has enough food for himself and his family for one day is required to donate to this charity after Ramadan, before the Eid prayer. Zakat al-Fitr is intended to provide food and happiness to the needy and impoverished on the day of Eid, as well as to cleanse the fasting individual of any transgressions or errors made throughout Ramadan. Depending on the area and the going rate in the market, the amount of Zakat al-Fitr is a certain quantity of food, such as dates, barley, wheat, or rice, or its equivalent in cash.

Sadaqah Al-Jariyah: This is a unique kind of charity that always provides benefits, such as constructing a road, a school, a hospital, a well, a mosque, planting a tree, or imparting information or skills to someone. Since the giver would continue to be rewarded for their generosity even after they pass away, sadaqah al-Jariyah is regarded as one of the finest types of giving.

CELEBRATING IN RAMADAN

The Joy, Sunnah, and Etiquette of Eid

Muslims celebrate Eid with delight and appreciation because it signifies the end of Ramadan, a month-long period of fasting, prayer, and almsgiving. Eid is also a day to observe the sunnah and manners of the Prophet Muhammad (peace be upon him), who instructed Muslims on how to observe the holiday with decency and decorum. Here are some ideas to help you comprehend and value the sunnah and etiquette of Eid, as well as the celebration of joy and thankfulness:

- The happiness and appreciation of Eid: Eid is a day to show happiness and appreciation to Allah for all of His favors and bounties. Muslims express their happiness and thanks in the following ways:
- By thanking Allah for allowing them to finish the month of Ramadan, they praise and honor Him by saying the takbir (Allahu akbar, Allah is the Greatest) from the evening of Eid till the Eid prayer.

- Honoring the event and expressing satisfaction by dressing in fresh or clean clothing, putting on perfume, and grooming oneself in Islamic law.
- Sending love and goodwill to their family, friends, and neighbors by exchanging congrats and greetings, such as "Taqabbal Allahu minna wa minkum" (May Allah accept from us and you) or "Eid Mubarak" (Blessed Eid).
- As a method to spread the love and charity of Eid, parents and relatives should give money and presents to their kids and other family members, particularly the underprivileged.
- By the Prophet's (peace be upon him) sunnah, celebrating the completion of fasting by eating and drinking, particularly dates, before the Eid prayer.

The sunnah and manners of Eid: Eid is a day dedicated to adhering to the sunnah and manners of the Prophet Muhammad (peace be upon him), who instructed Muslims on how to conduct the Eid prayer and the celebration's customs politely and appropriately. Among the sunnah and eid customs are:

- Before attending the Eid prayer, take a ceremonial bath, or ghusl, to cleanse oneself and get ready for the prayer.

- Showing excitement and imitating the Prophet (peace be upon him) by arriving to the Eid prayer early, walking if at all feasible, and choosing an alternative route back.
- If at all feasible, do the Eid prayer outside in a field or a mosque courtyard to accommodate the vast crowd and adhere to the Prophet's (peace be upon him) sunnah.
- Taking in and applying the teachings of the Eid khutbah (sermon), which is delivered after the Eid prayer, to reap the benefits of the imam's knowledge and counsel.
- To preserve the spirit and holiness of Eid, treat others with kindness, gentleness, and forgiveness and abstain from disagreements, conflicts, and transgressions.

Eid Customs and Activities

Eid is a day to rejoice and give thanks to Allah for all of His favors and bounties. Muslims express their thankfulness and delight by:

- Reciting the Takbir, which means "Allahu akbar, Allah is the Greatest," is a way to thank and praise Allah for allowing them to finish the Ramadan fast, from the evening of Eid till the Eid prayer.

- Honoring the event and expressing satisfaction by dressing in fresh or clean clothing, putting on perfume, and grooming oneself by Islamic law.
- Sending love and goodwill to their family, friends, and neighbors by exchanging congrats and greetings, such as "Taqabbal Allahu minna wa minkum" (May Allah accept from us and you) or "Eid Mubarak" (Blessed Eid).
- Distributing presents and cash to their kids and family members, particularly the underprivileged and destitute, to spread the happiness and giving of Eid.
- In accordance (peace be upon him) sunnah, celebrating the completion of fasting by eating and drinking, particularly on dates, before the Eid prayer.

The Reflections and Lessons of Eid

Eid is a day to apply the teachings and lessons learned during Ramadan to the remainder of the year. Among the insights and teachings from Eid are:

- It serves as a reminder of the significance of fasting and its advantages, which include thankfulness, self-control, discipline, and empathy. To preserve the spirit and benefits of fasting, Muslims should continue to fast willingly on other days, such as Mondays and Thursdays, the six days of Shawwal, or the day of Arafah. Since the Quran was revealed during the month of Ramadan, it is a celebration of the Quran and its teachings. Throughout the year, Muslims should seek the wisdom and kindness of the Quran by reciting, studying, and acting upon it.

- Muslims from all nations, ethnicities, and backgrounds gather to pray and rejoice, serving as a testament to the diversity and togetherness of the Muslim community. The ties of brothers and sisterhood should be maintained by Muslims, and they should recognize and value the distinctions between them.

- It is an example of Islam's kindness and generosity, as Muslims share their money and enjoyment with others and donate zakat and sadaqah to the underprivileged. Muslims should uphold their moral and social duties while continuing to be kind, helpful, and giving to others.

GLOSSARY

The definitions and pronunciations of some frequently used Arabic terms and phrases throughout the guide are provided below. Be aware that the pronunciation could differ somewhat based on the speaker's accent and dialect.

- As-salaam alaikum, or "peace be upon you," is a frequent greeting among Muslims. It is expressed as السلام عليكم. "And peace be upon you too" (Wa alaikum as-salaam) is the answer, وعليكم السلام.

The phrase "Sabah al-khair (صباح الخير) is used to welcome someone in the morning. صباح النور (Sabah al-noor) is the answer, meaning "morning of light".

- مرحبا (Marhaban): This is a common greeting that signifies "hello" and may be used at any time of day. مرحبا (Marhaban) is the same reaction.

- Ma'a as-salaah مع السلامة: This is a typical method of saying "goodbye" and it signifies "with peace". "May God protect you" is the answer, "الله يسلمك" (Allah yusallimak).

The Arabic word نعم (Na'am) signifies "yes" and is used to concur or confirm something. "No" is denoted by لا (La), the opposite.

The word "okay" (حسنا) in Hasanan is used to convey acceptance or approval of something. It also has the meanings "fine" or "well".

- من فضلك (Min fadlik): This is a polite way of saying "please" or making an offer. Min fadliki, or من فضلكِ, is the feminine version.

- Shukran: This represents "thank you" and is used to convey appreciation or thanks. عفوا (Afwan) is the reply, meaning "Don't mention it" or "You're welcome".

- "I'm sorry" is expressed with the phrase "انا اسف" (Ana asef). انا اسفة is the feminine version (Ana asefah). The reply is معلش (Ma'alesh), which translates to "Never mind" or "Okayokay".

- "I don't know" (La a'aref): This phrase is used to convey ignorance or doubt. لا أعرف is the feminine version (La a'arefah).

- أين الحمامآ (Ayna al-hammam?): This is a helpful question to ask when you need to use the toilet. It means "Where is the bathroom?" Usually, the reaction consists of pointing or providing instructions.

- آ أين محطة الخدمة؟ "Where is the service station?" is a helpful question to ask when you need to refuel your automobile or obtain assistance (Ayna mahattat al-khidmah?). Usually, the reaction consists of pointing or providing instructions.

- مساعدة! (Musa'adah!): This phrase, which translates to "help!" is used to request aid or attention in an emergency or other distressing circumstance. Usually, the answer is asking ماذا؟ متَ. (An maza tatahadath?), which translates to "Are are you talking about?" or عن ماذا تتحدث؟, which translates to "What happened?"

"انا لا اتكلم العربية" The phrase "I don't speak Arabic" (Ana la atakallam al-Arabiya) is used to let someone know that you are not proficient in the language.

CONCLUSION

We hope that this book, which has concluded, has been a helpful guide for you as you learn about and put the many facets of Ramadan into practice. For Muslims, Ramadan is a fortunate and holy month as it is the month of Eid, the Quran, fasting, prayer, and charitable giving. It is a time to cleanse our spirits, strengthen our faith, learn more, and spread our blessings to others throughout Ramadan. Ramadan is also a season for introspection, sin-repentance, and intention-renewal.

We hope that this book has made it easier for you to comprehend the meaning, guidelines, customs, and benefits of praying, fasting, reading the Quran, giving zakat, and celebrating Eid. We hope that this book has encouraged you to emulate the sunnah and the teachings of the Prophet Muhammad (peace be upon him), who was the most giving and excellent of instructors. We also hope that this book has given you some ideas, methods, and tools to help you have a more successful and pleasurable Ramadan.

We ask Allah to accept your good actions and fasting and to show you His forgiveness and kindness. We want Allah to provide you and your family wisdom, health, and joy throughout this Ramadan. We want Allah to grant you a happy and tranquil Eid. And we ask Allah to provide us the opportunity to observe many more Ramadans in the future.

We appreciate you taking the time to read this book.

As-salaam Alaikum, Peace be upon you.